I0448146

A Report to the Congress
in Accordance with Section 359
of the
Uniting and Strengthening America by Providing
Appropriate Tools Required to Intercept and Obstruct
Terrorism Act of 2001

(USA PATRIOT ACT)

Submitted by the Secretary of the U.S. Department of the Treasury
November 2002

TABLE OF CONTENTS

I. Executive Summary

On October 26, 2001, the President of the United States signed into law the Uniting and Strengthening America by Providing Appropriate Tools Required to Intercept and Obstruct Terrorism (USA PATRIOT Act) Act of 2001, Public Law 107-56. Section 359 of the USA PATRIOT Act requires:

> Section 359 – Reporting of Suspicious Activities by Underground Banking Systems
> (d) REPORT – Not later than 1 year after the date of enactment of this Act, the Secretary of the Treasury shall report to Congress on the need for any additional legislation relating to persons who engage as a business in an informal money transfer system or any network of people who engage as a business in facilitating the transfer of money domestically or internationally outside of the conventional financial institutions system, counter money laundering and regulatory controls relating to underground money movement and banking systems, including whether the threshold for the filing of suspicious activity reports under section 5318(g) of title 31, United States Code, should be lowered in the case of such systems.

The Secretary of the Treasury submits this report in accordance with the above requirement. Based on fieldwork and analysis of data gathered to date, the following preliminary findings are presented:

- Existing Bank Secrecy Act (BSA) regulations are applicable to the U.S.-based operators of informal value transfer systems.

- Current research does not suggest an immediate need for additional legislation, nor does it suggest a need to change the threshold for the filing of Suspicious Activity Reports.

- The adequacy of the existing BSA rules should be reexamined over the course of Treasury's multi-year effort to enhance regulatory compliance among the operators of informal value transfer systems.

- The law enforcement and regulatory communities should undertake a comprehensive program to enhance their knowledge concerning the range of mechanisms used in informal value transfer systems in order to better understand them and to determine whether they think that any additional legislation is needed.

The BSA, the primary anti-money laundering statute in the United States, includes provisions that apply to informal value transfer systems. Under the BSA, any person or group of persons who transfers money as a business is defined as a Money Services Business (MSB). These entities are defined as MSBs whether or not they transfer money on a regular basis, and whether or not they are an organized business concern.

The MSB class of financial institutions includes conventional entities with global reach such as Western Union and Thomas Cook. It also includes the types of informal or unconventional entities operating outside of the mainstream financial system, such as hawala, hundi, fei ch'ien, hoe kuan, hui k'aun, and many others. Historically, these informal entities have been labeled by various terms including "alternative remittance systems," "underground banks," and "informal value transfer systems."

Pursuant to the current MSB regulations, these businesses must register with the Financial Crimes Enforcement Network, conduct customer identification procedures for certain transactions, and maintain financial records. They are also required to file Currency Transaction Reports (CTRs) and Suspicious Activity Reports (SARs).

There are many uncertainties and complex issues associated with this segment of the financial industry. Treasury will therefore work closely with law enforcement, regulators, and the financial community to gain a fuller understanding of these informal networks and how they interact with the more formal financial industry. As Treasury continues to study and to address these issues, it will remain open to considering new legislation to reduce the vulnerability of MSBs in general, and informal value transfer systems in particular, to money laundering and terrorist financing. The attached appendices provide a more in-depth analysis of the data that has been gathered relating to informal value transfer systems.

II.   Research Methodology

The Financial Crimes Enforcement Network (FinCEN) was directed to carry out this study and staff[1] framed their research in the context of the following interrelated issues:

- The unique law enforcement and regulatory challenges associated with informal, unconventional, or underground money transfer mechanisms.

- The scope and application of the existing regulatory scheme with regard to businesses that facilitate the transfer of money domestically or internationally (to include persons who engage as a business in an informal money transfer system or any network of people who engage as a business in facilitating the transfer of money).

- The effectiveness of the existing money transmitter regulatory scheme with respect to these informal systems (to gauge the technical adequacy of the regulations, as well industry compliance).

---

[1]   FinCEN staff conducted interviews with federal, state, local, and foreign law enforcement personnel, and with representatives from the Federal Reserve Board, the Federal Reserve Bank of New York, the International Monetary Fund (IMF), and the World Bank. FinCEN staff also interviewed several providers of informal money transfer services, consulted with an academic expert in the field, and mined data collected pursuant to the BSA.

III. Background on Informal Value Transfer Systems

Informal Value Transfer Systems (IVTS) is a term used to describe those money or value transfer systems that operate informally to transfer money as a business. In the past, some of these informal networks have been labeled by various terms including "alternative remittance systems" and "underground banks." Within the broad realm of informal institutions there exist more detailed descriptors for specific value transfer mechanisms, such as hawala, hundi, fei ch'ien, hoe kuan, hui k'aun, and many others. For the purpose of consistency and inclusiveness, IVTS is the primary term of art used in this report. (See Appendix A for examples of IVTS mechanisms.)

U.S. citizens and persons residing in this country from nations in which the use of IVTS is commonplace use the system for various reasons. In countries lacking a stable financial sector or containing substantial areas not served by formal financial institutions, IVTS may be the only method for conducting financial transactions. For example, foreign aid money going to Afghanistan is being disbursed through IVTS due to a lack of a banking infrastructure. Individuals and organizations often use IVTS due to the existence of inadequate payments systems, to avoid foreign exchange or capital controls, and when the formal financial sector is not readily accessible, significantly more expensive, or more difficult to navigate.

The international flows of IVTS are most likely staggering, but quantification with any certainty is currently impossible. An IMF/World Bank estimate that is likely on the conservative side and only covers select countries puts annual worldwide IVTS transfers at tens of billions of dollars.

In order to better understand this issue, FinCEN looked closely at the workings of the hawala system, a widely used form of IVTS. Hawala means "transfer" in Arabic and the system works by transferring money without actually moving it. The basic hawala transaction involves a sender, two trusted intermediaries, and a recipient. For example, a U.S. resident who wants to send money to a friend in another jurisdiction (Country B) would give it to a U.S. hawaladar,[2] who typically gives the sender a code or identification mechanism. The U.S. hawaladar then contacts a local hawaladar in Country B by telephone, fax, or e-mail, and the sender contacts the intended recipient to convey the code. The local hawaladar in Country B then delivers the specified funds to the recipient upon presentation of the code. The hawaladar charges a flat fee, a commission, or may alternatively or in addition, profit from the exchange rate differential between the official and black market price of U.S. dollars in Country B. The accounts between the two operators may be settled various ways including through compensatory payments (i.e., when someone from Country B sends money to the U.S.), conventional wire transfers or checks, physical movement of money (by courier), invoice manipulation or other trade-based mechanisms, and the trade/smuggling of gold and precious gems. (See Appendix B for illustrations of these techniques.)

---

[2] The term hawaladar refers to a hawala dealer or provider of hawala money transfer services.

Even this brief description highlights some of the key similarities and differences between IVTS and formal value transfer mechanisms. While the primary transfer between the sender and the recipient contains some unconventional elements (by U.S. standards), the far greater differences occur on the back end, or settlement side of IVTS.

While it appears that the majority of IVTS activity is legitimate in purpose,[3] these systems have been used to facilitate the financing of terrorism and in furtherance of criminal activities. For this reason, many governments have begun to look at this issue in terms of the need for regulatory and legal controls and in terms of their ability to conduct successful financial investigations in cases where IVTS has been used.

In order to make a judgment about whether the U.S. may need additional legislation at this time to address informal value transfer systems, it is first necessary to understand the present legal and regulatory regime. FinCEN's analysis focused on the relevance of existing regulations in the context of IVTS and whether these are adequate to deal with the unique challenges presented by IVTS.

IV. Existing Regulations for Informal Value Transfer Systems, Including Suspicious Activity Reporting

The BSA[4] authorizes the Secretary of the Treasury to impose on financial institutions a variety of recordkeeping and reporting requirements that are deemed useful to criminal, tax, and regulatory enforcement, and in the conduct of intelligence and counter-intelligence activities relating to international terrorism.

FinCEN administers the BSA on behalf of Treasury and has adopted a broad interpretation of the regulations with regard to their application to money transmitters. In 1999, FinCEN amended the regulatory definition of a money transmitter to include "any person, whether or not licensed or required to be licensed, who engages as a business in accepting currency, or funds denominated in currency, and transmits the currency or funds, or the value of the currency or funds, by any means through a financial agency or institution, a Federal Reserve Bank or other facility of one or more Federal Reserve Banks, the Board of Governors of the Federal Reserve System, or both, or an electronic funds network" or "any other person engaged as a business in the transfer of funds."[5]

Section 359(a) of the Patriot Act amended the definition of money transmitter to encompass "any person who engages as a business in an informal money transfer system or any network of people who engage as a business in facilitating the transfer of money domestically or internationally outside of the conventional financial institution system." These amendments make clear that under U.S. law all money transfer remitters, including

---

[3] IVTS traditionally serves the purpose of remitting funds of expatriate communities to their home countries.
[4] See 31 U.S.C. 5311 et seq.
[5] See 31 CFR 103.11(uu)(5).

those that operate on an informal basis, or outside the scope of the conventional financial sector, are subject to the BSA.

Money transmitters, as currently understood, are one of a number of non-bank financial institutions that, for purposes of the BSA, are grouped within the category called MSBs. This category of institutions also includes check cashers, currency exchangers, and issuers, sellers, and redeemers of traveler's checks, money orders, and stored value.[6]

As of December 31, 2001, all MSB principals (except the U.S. Postal Service, federal, state, or local governmental units, and issuers and sellers of stored value) were required to register with FinCEN. The registration form requires that the MSB provide not only contact information, but also identify its owner or controlling person, provide a governmentally-issued identification number for that person, and identify the company's primary transaction account. These registration records are provided online to FinCEN's Gateway[7] partners for use in their investigations.

Although agents of MSBs are not independently required to register, FinCEN's regulations require all MSB principals to maintain a list of their agents and to make the list available on request to FinCEN or any other appropriate law enforcement agency.[8] The agent list must include, in addition to identifying information (name, address, telephone number), a listing of the months in which the agent's gross transactions for the previous year exceeded $100,000, the name and address of any depository institution at which the agent maintains a transaction account, and the number of branches or subagents the agent has.

Any MSB that fails to register with FinCEN, or files false or incomplete information in the registration statement, is subject to civil penalties of $5,000 per day while the violation continues. In addition, under 18 U.S.C. 1960, any person who knowingly engages in a money transmitting business, and has failed to register and/or comply with FinCEN's registration regulations, may be subject to up to five years' imprisonment.

All MSBs, including those that could be characterized as IVTS, must obtain and verify customer identity and record beneficiary information for funds transfers of more than $3,000.[9] There are also separate recordkeeping requirements applicable to the sale of MSB products, such as traveler's checks and money orders, as well as to currency exchange transactions.[10] These records must be maintained for five years.[11] In addition,

---

[6] The definition of every category of MSB other than a money transmitter has a threshold requirement that the business engage in a transaction within the category (currency exchange, check cashing, etc.) in the amount of $1,000 for any one customer in one day. There is no threshold requirement for money transmitters.

[7] FinCEN's Gateway system enables federal, state, and local law enforcement agencies to have direct, online access to records filed under the BSA. See 2002 National Money Laundering Strategy, at 53.

[8] See 31 CFR 103.41.

[9] See 31 CFR 103.33(f).

[10] See 31 CFR 103.29, 103.37.

transactions in currency of more than $10,000 are subject to detailed recordkeeping requirements to support the filing of CTRs.[12]

MSBs are also subject to the SAR rule. As is the case with all MSBs, IVTS operators are required to file with FinCEN a SAR with respect to any transaction over $2,000 that it knows, suspects, or has reason to suspect involves funds from illegal activity or is designed to conceal their origin, is designed to evade BSA obligations, or has no apparent business or law purpose.[13]

In addition to routine recordkeeping and reporting, FinCEN's regulations also authorize the imposition of further reporting requirements where needed to carry out the purposes of the BSA regulations or to prevent the evasion of the BSA's recordkeeping and reporting requirements.[14] Such additional requirements are imposed by means of what is known as a geographic targeting order (GTO)[15] and may be applied to any domestic financial institution or group of domestic financial institutions in a geographic area, as well as persons participating in transactions subject to the order.

A GTO can be as detailed as requiring reporting of all transactions in currency and/or monetary instruments, or of classes of transactions, equal to or exceeding an amount specified in the GTO. Among other things, this regulation permits Treasury to require reporting at a much lower threshold than otherwise required by its rules. For example, GTOs have been successfully applied against money transmitters in two metropolitan areas that were heavily used by drug traffickers. The GTOs required records to be maintained and reports filed of all transactions over $750. The GTOs resulted in the gathering of useful information for law enforcement and several successful money laundering and structuring prosecutions.

Persons willfully violating any BSA reporting or recordkeeping requirement are subject to civil and criminal penalties and imprisonment under 31 U.S.C. 5321-22. Willful violations of any requirement imposed under a GTO are similarly subject to civil and criminal sanctions.

As noted above, Section 1960 of Title 18 makes it a crime to operate an MSB in the absence of compliance with FinCEN's registration requirements. It also makes it a crime to operate an MSB in the absence of compliance with applicable state licensing

---

[11] See 31 CFR 103.38.

[12] See 31 CFR 103.28. In addition, any person who physically transports or causes the transport of over $10,000 in currency or monetary instruments into or out of the United States must file a Report of International Transportation of Currency or Monetary Instruments (CMIR) with FinCEN. See 31 CFR 103.23.

[13] See 31 CFR 103.20. FinCEN has published a notice of proposed rulemaking to add a fourth category to the MSB SAR rule for transactions that involve use of the MSB to facilitate criminal activity. See 67 FR 64075 (October 17, 2002). Issuers of traveler's checks and money orders (as opposed to sellers or redeemers), are subject to SAR requirement at a $5,000 threshold.

[14] See 31 CFR 103.26.

[15] Issued under the BSA, a GTO is used to impose stricter reporting and recordkeeping requirements on specified financial service providers in a certain geographical area for a limited time period.

requirements.[16] As amended by the Patriot Act, Section 1960(b)(1)(A) specifically provides that a conviction for failure to comply with a state licensing requirement does not require proof that the defendant knew of the state licensing requirement. However, there is no comparable language in Section 1960(b)(1)(B) for a defendant who fails to comply with the MSB registration requirement and regulations, which could lead a court to infer that such proof is required under that subsection.

Other criminal laws potentially applicable to IVTS providers include Sections 2339A and 2339B of Title 18, which prohibit the providing of material support to a terrorist or to a designated terrorist organization.[17] In addition, these crimes, like the vast majority of federal white-collar crimes and offenses traditionally associated with organized crime, serve as predicate acts for the crime of money laundering under the money laundering statutes, 18 U.S.C. 1956 and 1957. Section 1956 prohibits the conduct of a "financial transaction" involving proceeds known to derive from some "specified unlawful activity." A transaction is a "financial transaction" under the statute if it involves monetary instruments, the movement of funds, the transfer of title to property, or the use of a financial institution. To be guilty of money laundering under section 1956, the defendant must act with the intent to: (1) promote the carrying on of a specified unlawful activity; (2) engage in tax fraud; (3) conceal or disguise the nature, location, source, ownership, or control of the property; or (4) avoid a transaction-reporting requirement. For example, section 1956 bars "smurfing" – the practice of intentionally structuring transactions to avoid reporting requirements by splitting the total amount of funds available for deposit into amounts below the $10,000 reporting threshold.

Section 1957 prohibits the engagement in a "monetary transaction" involving property that is known to be derived from a criminal offense, and that is actually derived from a "specified unlawful activity," of a value greater than $10,000. The term "monetary transaction" is defined broadly to cover almost any transaction by, through, or to a financial institution, including the deposit, withdrawal, transfer, or exchange of funds or a monetary instrument. Unlike section 1956, section 1957 does not require the defendant to know that the property was derived from a particular "specified unlawful activity" or a "specified unlawful activity" in general. Rather, section 1957 requires the defendant to know only that the property was derived from some criminal offense. Therefore, a defendant cannot rely on willful blindness to avoid liability under section 1957.

---

[16] Most, but not all states, have such licensing requirements. In the Money Laundering Suppression Act of 1994, Pub. L. 103-325, 108 Stat. 2160, Congress recommended that the States enact uniform laws to regulate MSBs. In response, the National Conference of Commissioners on Uniform State Laws (NCCUSL) has promulgated a model law regulating MSBs, which it recommended that all States enact. See Uniform Money Services Act (2000) (available on http://www.law.upenn.edu/bll/ulc/ulc_frame.htm). The NCCUSL recently created a study committee to determine whether the Uniform Money Services Act needs to be revised or updated in light of the events of September 11 and subsequent developments in the field.

[17] These statutes were enacted in 1994 and 1996. The first conviction under Sec. 2339B occurred in June 2002. United States v. Hammoud, No. 3:00CR147-MU (W.D. N.C.).

Finally, 18 U.S.C. 2 prohibits anyone from aiding and abetting an offense against the United States. This statute would apply, for example, to an IVTS operator that knowingly offered material assistance to anyone committing a federal crime.[18]

V.   Law Enforcement Challenges

To determine whether additional legislation or regulation is needed to deal with the risks posed by IVTS, FinCEN's study reviewed the challenges IVTS poses to law enforcement in conducting financial investigations. Although law enforcement has not yet had a great deal of exposure to IVTS, the experience to date demonstrates that the problems do not arise from the lack of pertinent statutory or regulatory tools. Rather, the challenges to effective law enforcement in this area stem from the need for stepped up compliance, education, and cooperation. These challenges are discussed below.

As authorities have been intensifying their efforts to block terrorists from obtaining funds in the United States and elsewhere, more focused attention has been devoted to hawala and other IVTS. In several countries, hawala has operated in parallel with formal financial institutions or as a substitute or alternative for them. IVTS-type networks are used by persons in the U.S. to send money or gifts to their friends and relatives residing in Asian, African, and Middle Eastern countries.

While it appears that most clients of IVTS legitimately earn their money and try to assist their extended families, criminals have also used these networks to launder dirty money, make illicit payments, and commit other offenses, such as tax evasion and customs violations. Dealing with illegal hawala providers and their networks represents a serious challenge to U.S. law enforcement agencies for many reasons. Of particular concern is the need for increased expertise in understanding the complexities of IVTS.

Certain common characteristics may often create extensive obstacles for law enforcement. These include: (1) non-standardized or non-existent recordkeeping and know-your-customer type of practices; (2) frequent commingling of hawala with other business activities, including commodity trading or smuggling, when transactions pass through jurisdictions with porous borders or cash-based economies; (3) language and cultural barriers; and (4) inconsistent laws and regulations at the international and domestic levels.

Recordkeeping Practices

Hawala ledgers are often insubstantial and in idiosyncratic shorthand. Initials or numbers that are meaningful to the hawaladar are useless if they reveal nothing about transactions, amounts, time, and names of people or organizations. Personal ledgers are often destroyed within a short period of time, especially in countries where *hawala* is criminalized.

---

[18] See U.S. v. Levy, 969 F.2d 136 (5th Cir. 1992) (upholding conviction for aiding and abetting failure to report currency transactions).

In some cases, particularly when hawaladars know that their clients are breaking the law, no notes or records are kept at all. In other cases, hawaladars may serve customers without asking many questions about their true identity, the origin of their money, or the reason for the transfer. In such cases, even if providers decided to cooperate with authorities, they would have no knowledge or useful information to share. Without records or some documentary basis, there is virtually no paper trail and very little that investigators can pursue, thus leaving them at a dead end in their efforts to build a case.

On the other hand, investigators sometimes end up finding masses of records, ledgers, or notes kept by IVTS providers. However, they may be maintained in ways that are hard to decipher without the cooperation of those who created the records. Sometimes the notes are kept in foreign languages or in initials and codes.

In other instances, the transaction may involve third party accounts of individuals or companies within the same country or a number of other countries. Nominee accounts, sometimes referred to as "Benami,"[19] effectively stop the money trail, as evident from investigations of banking, financial, and trade-related misconduct.

In the end, much of the paper trail might surface, but it becomes a difficult task to interpret and reconstruct it accurately. The task of putting everything together for a case becomes time consuming and complicated, and may require the cooperation of hawala providers or controllers in other jurisdictions, thus requiring significant resources.

As noted in the previous section, IVTS operators are money transmitters under the BSA, and FinCEN's recordkeeping rules are applicable to them. Achieving better compliance does not call for additional legislation or regulation, but for increased outreach, education, and enforcement.

Mixing of Businesses

Another challenge for law enforcement is proving criminal offenses and intent when commingling of funds takes place. For example, businesses operating with substantial amounts of cash or involving high turnover make it very easy to hide illegal hawala deals by creating, for instance, "black holes" domestically and overseas. These black holes are formed by withdrawing cash pooled by IVTS providers, depositing it in different accounts at various intervals, and at various financial institutions (banks, brokerages, and others), and/or using the funds to purchase commodities that then can be traded in the U.S. or internationally. It is virtually impossible to match cash withdrawals with other deposits and trade transactions when the amounts are comparatively small.

In other cases, hawala businesses interface with financial institutions (e.g., they may have bank or brokerage accounts, currency exchangers, offer telephone and fax services, send wires, engage in real estate deals). A currency exchanger in a given country could

---

[19] *"Benami"* or nominee accounts are culturally accepted in ethnic groups that also engage in hawala. Because the true beneficiary of a transaction is not the person under whose name the transaction takes place, it is very hard to identify the owners of criminal proceeds and people who engage in illegal activities.

send and receive wire transfers for a hawala customer via one or two foreign banks. When the funds are booked into certain types of correspondent accounts at U.S.-based banks (i.e., those that are not payable-through accounts), the trail becomes blurred as the funds move from an institutional account not identified with any individual before finally being transmitted to the ultimate intended recipient. However, this issue is not unique to IVTS, but is a function of the realities of correspondent banking.[20]

Again, these are not issues that require additional legislation or regulation. Rather, addressing these issues requires education and cooperation among regulators, law enforcement, and the financial community. Therefore, it is important for the law enforcement and regulatory communities to educate financial institutions about the typologies associated with IVTS. It is necessary that bank officials, credit card companies, brokerages, money exchanges, transmitters, and others be made familiar with illicit IVTS patterns, recognize them, and report them as suspicious.

Language and Cultural Barriers

U.S. law enforcement often is faced with language and cultural barriers when trying to communicate with suspects, identify suspicious transactions, interpret evidence, and conduct undercover operations. For instance, when hawala ledgers are found, it may be impossible for law enforcement to understand their contents and underlying transactions. Therefore, the cooperation of IVTS providers is often essential in deciphering these records (as in cases of accounting fraud or records of drug traffickers). However, such cooperation may not always be forthcoming, if ethnic, cultural, or other sensitivities are misunderstood or ignored by law enforcement.

On the other hand, too much focus on particular ethnic groups or cultural practices may divert attention from any potential intersection or collaboration across ethnic lines. For example, there have been cases in which persons of one ethnic background have used systems prevalent in another culture or cultures. Outreach efforts by law enforcement into the affected communities can enhance the efforts to obtain their cooperation and improve our understanding of how IVTS is used and abused.

Inconsistency in Laws and Regulations

Differences in laws and regulations internationally also pose a major challenge to law enforcement. (See Appendix D for a description of international regulatory approaches). When hawala operates through jurisdictions with strict secrecy regulations, the investigative task is further complicated and cooperation is lessened. Bank secrecy, corporate secrecy, and attorney-client privilege make the investigator's task difficult. Sometimes, a vicious circle prevents law enforcement agents from completing their task. In order to obtain information from such jurisdictions, evidence of wrongdoing is

---

[20] Pursuant to Section 312 of the USA Patriot Act, regulations have been proposed that would require U.S. financial institutions offering correspondent accounts to perform due diligence and, in appropriate circumstances, enhanced due diligence on their correspondents. See 67 FR 37,736 (May 30, 2002) and 67 FR 48,348 (July 23, 2002).

required; however, access to information in those jurisdictions is critical in obtaining that evidence in the first place. Addressing these challenges requires multilateral, rather than unilateral, action, as discussed below.

VI.   **Examples of Counter-Measures Being Developed**

As noted above, the challenges faced by law enforcement in confronting IVTS do not currently appear to require a legislative solution, but appear amenable to counter-measures by the regulatory and law enforcement communities that involve compliance efforts, education, and outreach, and increased cooperation between and among government and the financial sector. In this section, we discuss some examples of the more promising strategies that are being developed to enable law enforcement to deal with financial investigations involving IVTS. The lesson from these examples is that the existing legislative framework offers appropriate tools and opportunities to effectuate law enforcement counter-measures aimed at the abuse of IVTS.

During its research for this report, FinCEN had an opportunity to observe several developing counter-measure strategies being applied in different regions through the United States. These strategies are directed toward:

❑   enhancing the transparency of IVTS operations;

❑   bringing the IVTS providers into the BSA regulatory structure;

❑   obtaining cooperation in interpreting relevant records and further understanding of IVTS mechanisms and customer activity;

❑   revealing trends and patterns of typical versus atypical suspect transactions;

❑   revealing ancillary or mixed business associations;

❑   disrupting and prosecuting immediate threats, while sending a message to other IVTS entities to comply with regulatory requirements;

❑   disrupting and turning over couriers associated with IVTS; and

❑   working with the financial sector to better monitor and detect suspicious IVTS activities. Examples of some of these strategies are discussed below.

Visits to California, New York, and Puerto Rico by representatives from FinCEN revealed successful outreach strategies being pursued in several regions by both law enforcement and regulatory authorities, which are aimed at the IVTS sector. These strategies are designed to enhance cooperation with IVTS providers in interpreting their records, and to learning about their operations, mechanisms, and customer transaction profiles. There has been substantial support for such outreach strategies among multiple agency representatives from many different regions of the country.

13

Law enforcement also is engaged in the extensive review of SARs filed on IVTS-related activity. Currently, the New York High Intensity Money Laundering and Related Financial Crime Area (HIFCA) has developed a SAR review strategy that encompasses an extensive review of SARs followed by categorizing the suspicious activity. Each level of that review involves correlated searches with other types of suspicious activity with other law enforcement sources of information. Following this analytical process, records are created in various law enforcement indices and then further examined for possible investigative development at regular multi-agency and multi-district SAR meetings. These meetings also included the participation of regulatory agencies and prosecutors.

Federal officials interviewed in another region of the country have applied existing regulatory provisions to derive an innovative triad approach for potential prosecutions of CMIR and bulk smuggling violations (31 U.S.C. Sections 5316 and 5332, respectively). This approach emphasizes the importance of law enforcement authorities being able to apply currency smuggling related statutes to investigations that might involve couriers linked to IVTS operations. If a courier associated with an IVTS-type business is detected at the border with more than $10,000 and an apparent intent to conceal the money, both CMIR violation charges and bulk cash smuggling charges may be applied. If the suspect declares that the funds are not his/her own but rather he/she is moving them on behalf of someone else, the suspect can be subject to Section 1960 charges for operating as an unlicensed money transmitter. In addition, if the courier is working for a particular business (i.e., a suspected IVTS operation), then CMIR, bulk-cash smuggling, and, potentially, Section 1960 charges may be filed against the source business and its owners.

Law enforcement is also making a concerted effort to work more closely with the larger financial community to assist banks and other depository institutions in becoming more familiar with transactions that may indicate suspicious IVTS activity. FinCEN believes this type of outreach to the financial community is critical in view of the extensive interface between IVTS and formal banking services. The cases included in this report (see Appendix C) illustrate that SARs play a significant role.

An example of a state-initiated strategy is the current program being developed by the New York State Attorney General's Office, in conjunction with a multi-agency task force, to identify regionally based IVTS operations, particularly in the terrorist financing context.

The goals of this program include:

❑ identifying, within the region, unlicensed money transmitters operating hawala-type businesses and feeding the information into a central database for further tracking and review for both law enforcement and intelligence purposes;

❑ determining methods of operation and identifying any associated ("second tier") businesses;

- ❏ prosecuting individuals violating state law and, wherever possible (based upon corroborating information, such as intelligence checks and leads, informants, bank record reviews) identifying investigative leads to terrorist activities;

- ❏ removing and/or disrupting immediate threats and thus sending a message to other IVTS entities to comply with regulatory requirements; and

- ❏ further identifying IVTS activity trends, patterns, operations, records, and customer transaction profiles.

These strategies all rely on the existing legislative and regulatory structure governing MSBs. They are examples of how the law enforcement and regulatory communities can carefully tailor existing regulatory tools to cope with the challenges posed by IVTS.

VII. Recommendations

The U.S. approach of regulating informal value transfer activity is preferable to outlawing the activity altogether, a course chosen by some nations. Attempting to outlaw IVTS ultimately deprives law enforcement of potentially valuable information and drives the informal remittance providers further "underground." Outlawing the activity also deprives the mostly law-abiding IVTS customers of the primary channel through which they transfer funds.

In addition, the U.S. approach to regulation is consistent with emerging international standards such as the Special Recommendations on Terrorist Financing, issued in November 2001, by the Financial Action Task Force (FATF) on Money Laundering. The FATF's Special Recommendation VI on Alternative Remittance calls on nations to "take measures to ensure that persons or legal entities, including agents, that provide a service for the transmission of money or value, including transmission through an informal value transfer system or network, should be licensed or registered and subject to all the FATF Recommendations that apply to banks and non-bank financial institutions."

The U.S. approach is also consistent with the Abu Dhabi Declaration on hawala issued in May of this year in the United Arab Emirates, following a congress of government officials from more than 50 nations. The declaration calls on countries to "adopt the FATF recommendations in relation to remitters, including hawaladars and other alternative remittance providers," and to "designate competent supervisory authorities to monitor and enforce the application of these recommendations to hawaladars and other alternative remittance providers." The declaration goes on to say that, "the international community should remain seized with the issue and should continue to work individually and collectively to regulate the hawala system for legitimate commerce and to prevent its exploitation or misuse by criminals or others."

As described in this report, the BSA clearly provides the framework for comprehensive oversight of all U.S.-based money transmitters, including those characterized as IVTS. However, many of the requirements under the BSA framework are too new to adequately determine their effectiveness with respect to IVTS.

Treasury, therefore, believes it would be premature at this time to call for new legislation. Based on what we know so far, we appear to have the legislative and regulatory tools that we need. The primary problems are those of compliance, enforcement, education, and cooperation. Treasury accordingly recommends that U.S. efforts be focused on these areas, beginning with the effort to bring all money transmitters, IVTS or otherwise, into compliance with the existing regulatory regime.

Similarly, we believe it is premature to change the SAR threshold. The MSB SAR requirement is less than one year old—insufficient time to enable FinCEN to determine whether relevant activity is being captured by the current threshold.

Like the SAR requirement, the MSB registration requirement is less than one year old. Anecdotal evidence suggests that the compliance rate among IVTS providers is far lower than among more conventional types of MSBs. Further research should be undertaken by FinCEN to determine the accuracy of this evidence and how compliance can be maximized.

The compliance question will be critically important as Treasury continues to assess the adequacy of existing regulations. This is particularly relevant in relation to the recordkeeping and customer identification rules, both of which directly impact on the law enforcement and regulatory challenges presented by IVTS.

One of the key compliance issues identified through FinCEN's analysis is the fact that IVTS operators often maintain non-standardized records and do not exercise sound customer identification practices. Investigators, for example, sometimes find records, ledgers, or notes maintained in code, or in idiosyncratic shorthand, making it hard to decipher without the cooperation of the IVTS operator who created the records. In some cases, particularly when ITVS operators know or suspect that their clients are breaking the law, no notes or records are kept. In other cases, IVTS operators serve customers without asking questions about their true identity, the origin of their money, or the reason for the transfer. In most instances, the practices described above are violations of the existing regulatory requirements.

Other compliance issues arise from the practice of IVTS operators of pooling funds from numerous transactions. As previously noted, businesses operating with substantial amounts of cash (such as convenience stores) or involving high turnover make it very easy to hide illegal IVTS transactions through the commingling of funds (see page 11, supra). It is virtually impossible to match cash withdrawals with other deposits and trade transactions when the amounts are comparatively small.

Compliance by IVTS providers with the BSA's existing recordkeeping, customer identification, and reporting requirements may go a long way to address these problems and to enable investigators to "follow the money trail." For example, the problem of incomplete, coded, or illegible records may be addressed because inherent in the BSA's recordkeeping requirements is the requirement that the records be truthful, complete, and accurate.[21] Coded and illegible records do not meet this standard. The problem raised by the practice of aggregating customers' transactions before transmitting them through depository institutions is addressed by the requirement that individualized records must be maintained for each transmittal order, which includes, for customers other than established customers, the requirement that customer identity be verified and recorded.[22]

Reporting of suspicious activities by IVTS providers will give law enforcement an important window into, and an early warning system for, questionable activity in communities that may otherwise be difficult to penetrate. Finally, IVTS compliance with the BSA's CTR and CMIR requirements has the potential to aid substantially in detecting IVTS-related bulk cash smuggling and other currency-related crimes.

Education and outreach are the crucial ingredients to building capacity among legitimate IVTS providers who want to comply with the law and regulations. FinCEN is currently expanding its existing outreach program that already has resulted in the registration of over 11,000 MSB principals. The planning process for the expanded program, which will include the translation of educational materials into various languages, meetings with associations of business in affected communities, and, possibly, the use of focus groups, is underway.

Education is also critically needed within the law enforcement and regulatory communities, as there needs to be a greater understanding of how these systems operate. The dearth of technical knowledge is compounded by the fact that IVTS is used in the U.S. primarily among immigrant communities, which poses an additional challenge to investigators and regulators who may lack the language skills and cultural awareness necessary to operate in this environment. These types of barriers can limit the ability of authorities to communicate with IVTS operators and/or criminal suspects to interpret evidence or to conduct effective undercover operations. It is equally important to enhance the awareness of the formal financial industry regarding existing and continually emerging IVTS mechanisms that may interface with the formal banking sector, especially in the context of their performance of their due diligence and SAR obligations.

Finally, although we already know much about some types of IVTS and how they operate, there is still much that remains a mystery. Treasury, therefore, believes that there is a need for continued research, particularly with regard to understanding the range of mechanisms associated with the IVTS payment clearance mechanisms.

---

[21] See, e.g., Lowell Niebur & Co., Inc., 18 SEC 471, 475 (1945).
[22] FinCEN anticipates that, once the Section 326 rules for verification of identity are finalized for those financial institutions that maintain accounts for customers, the rules for verification of identity for the various transactions entered into by MSBs (including rules governing funds transmittal by both bank and nonbank financial institutions) will be amended as needed to be consistent with the Section 326 rules.

APPENDICES

APPENDIX	TITLE
A	Range of Existing and Continually Emerging IVTS Mechanisms and Mixes With Formal Banking Sector
B	Basic *Hawala* and Sample Account Settling
C	Developing Case Patterns
D	International Oversight Practices
E	Acknowledgments

Appendix A

Range of Existing and Continually Emerging IVTS Mechanisms and Mixes With Formal Banking Sector

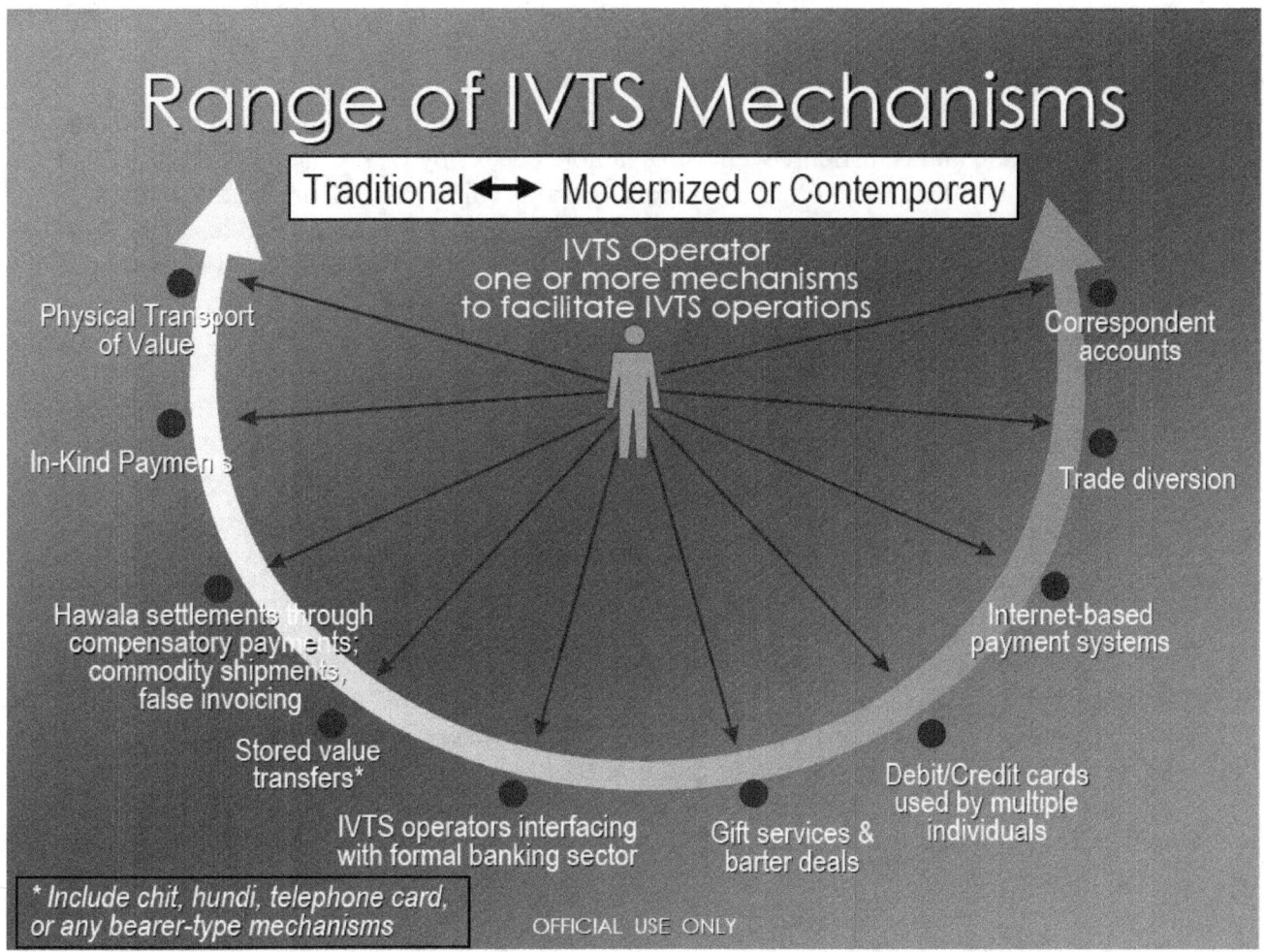

Broad Scope of IVTS Mechanisms

A primary finding resulting from the study is the need for law enforcement and regulatory authorities to be cognizant of the extensive and potentially complex (sometimes interfacing) nature of existing and continually emerging IVTS mechanisms, as the above graphic illustrates.

The following are examples of IVTS methods that, in and of themselves, may serve as mechanisms for transferring funds or value and sometimes interface with each other for settlement purposes:

1.   *False Invoicing of Exports or Imports* – This practice can help hawaladars balance their books. For instance, under-invoicing by $20,000, the hawaladar "sends" this amount to the importer of computer equipment, who will make profits higher by this amount upon resale of the goods. If the amounts are not excessive, they can easily "disappear" in otherwise legal trade. A $20,000 "mistake" in a $1-2 million trade is unlikely to raise suspicion, even if detected. Therefore, false invoicing can serve to be a stand-alone IVTS, part of a trade diversion scheme, or a means of tax evasion.

The detection of under-valuation or over-valuation of goods often requires inside information and is difficult even using sample checks by U.S. Customs Service (i.e., if medical, computer, and other equipment contains chips, drivers, or updated software versions, these can only be discovered if the equipment is opened up and subjected to the most thorough inspection). However, existing technologies may be used to overcome such difficulties. The U.S. Customs Service operates a relational database, developed in the early 1990s, that enables the analysis of data by country, port, manufacturers, importer, and commodity. That database is known as the Numerically Integrated Profiling System or NIPS. Investigators, using NIPS, have the ability to run samples against the database to help detect anomalies and thus provide leads regarding false-invoicing schemes.

In other cases, "payments" are made for goods that are not delivered, incorrectly described in the invoice, or returned after delivery is recorded. The payment does not appear to be connected to any unusual or suspicious activity.

2.   *Courier Services and Physical Transport* – Courier services and physical transport methods also can be used to transfer funds or other value and settle accounts amongst IVTS Providers. Cash has been found in everything from containers to suitcases. Money changers in the Middle East, who trade in currencies and therefore need the cash in place, also use couriers. Value can also be moved when IVTS Providers use cash to purchase easily movable commodities that can later be sold for cash at the final destination.

3.   *Correspondent Bank Accounts* – Certain types of correspondent accounts (such as "nostro" and "vostro")[23] may be used as the modern equivalent of a sophisticated 'hawala' moving more substantial amounts of value without the bank officials in the U.S., or even in other countries knowing the true identity of the customer. Access to the U.S. financial system is an added advantage to users of these mechanisms. This type of activity is particularly problematic in nesting or multiple levels of accounts, in which

---

[23] Nostro and vostro accounts are held by banks at other banks in foreign currencies and jurisdictions, where they have no presence themselves. For example, when bank A from country X needs to engage in U.S. dollar transactions but has no offices in the U.S., it may open a nostro (literally "our") account with a New York bank B. When bank B, on the other hand, wishes to engage in transactions denominated in the currency of country X but has no offices there, it will open a locally denominated account with bank A in that country. This would be a vostro account ("your account"). These are essentially clearing accounts that balance transactions between the two banks. Whereas a correspondent account is more of a one-way service, nostro/vostro accounts serve reciprocal interests and are like "mirror" accounts.

large numbers of institutional and individual accounts are consolidated through a network of banks.

4.   ***Gift and Money Transfer Services*** – Smaller amounts can also be transferred through easily available gift and money transfer services via special vouchers that can be bought through internet websites. Clients provide a credit card number to be charged for goods (such as flowers, food, or super market vouchers) to be received and/or used by a friend or relative elsewhere around the world.

5.   ***In-Kind Payments*** – Another practice that can be used independently, or as a settlement method, involves the provision of services or in-kind payments. For example, a travel agent sending groups to India may have someone pay all the expenses of the group, and make a payment to any account in the United States, or other account of the Indian provider.

6.   ***Debit and Credit Cards*** – These types of cards may be used by multiple individuals. Holders of bank or credit card accounts may have multiple cards on the same account and hand them over to other people, who may use the cards for withdrawals in other countries. Only the account holder may know who is taking the cash and for what purpose, and even the account holder may not know where the value goes next.

7.   ***Internet Payment Schemes*** – Similar, but often more complicated, alternatives involve internet companies that offer payments and money transfer services from within the U.S. or from overseas, including some based in secrecy or laxly regulated jurisdictions. Others facilitate payments and value transfers on the basis of gold deposits held in London, Zurich, or Dubai.

8.   ***Pre-paid Telephone Cards*** – These cards and any other instruments that effectively store value may be used for funds transfer.

9.   ***Trade Diversion Schemes*** – These schemes allow for hard-to-detect value transfers, the laundering of dirty money, as well as fast illegal profits. For example, Customer X (e.g., a front company based abroad) purchases legal goods at a discount (often up to 50 percent) from a U.S. manufacturer, and receives the goods via an intermediary in a third country. The goods are then diverted back (i.e., returned) to the United States. These goods are eventually sold to wholesalers in the U.S. by Customer X (or an intermediary) at a higher price. This price still represents though for the wholesalers a discount (e.g., 20 percent), and for Customer X the receipt of legal money anywhere on earth as proceeds of a legal sale. Buying a million dollars worth of goods for $500,000 and re-selling them for $800,000 in a couple of weeks generates a profit of $300,000 and clean funds for anyone to use.

Therefore, it is clear that IVTS can include a very wide range of methods – from very basic to extremely sophisticated methods. It is also important to note that in certain instances the interface of several types of IVTS include the finding of cross-ethnic

21

(middlemen) collaborations; the more interface used and the greater use of intermediaries, the harder it becomes to investigate a case or network.

IX.   *Mixing of IVTS Mechanisms with the Formal Banking Sector*

Our study has found few examples of "basic" hawala in the United States; that is, where value transfers occur without any interface with the formal banking sector. IVTS providers interface with the formal banking sector when they make deposits, engage in wire or other transfers, and manage ancillary businesses (e.g., travel agency, grocery store, jewelry store). In many of the cases reviewed, it became apparent that during the settlement process, the IVTS operator transferred funds through financial institutions on an aggregated basis when its cash pool reached a certain level. FinCEN has also observed IVTS providers who maintain bank accounts in order to obtain negotiable instruments, to wire funds domestically and overseas, and to draw on for the purchase of commodities/goods (the proceeds from sale of these commodities/goods were then used to remit money overseas on behalf of local IVTS customers). (See Case Synopses illustrated in Appendix C.)

Basic Hawala and Sample Account Settling

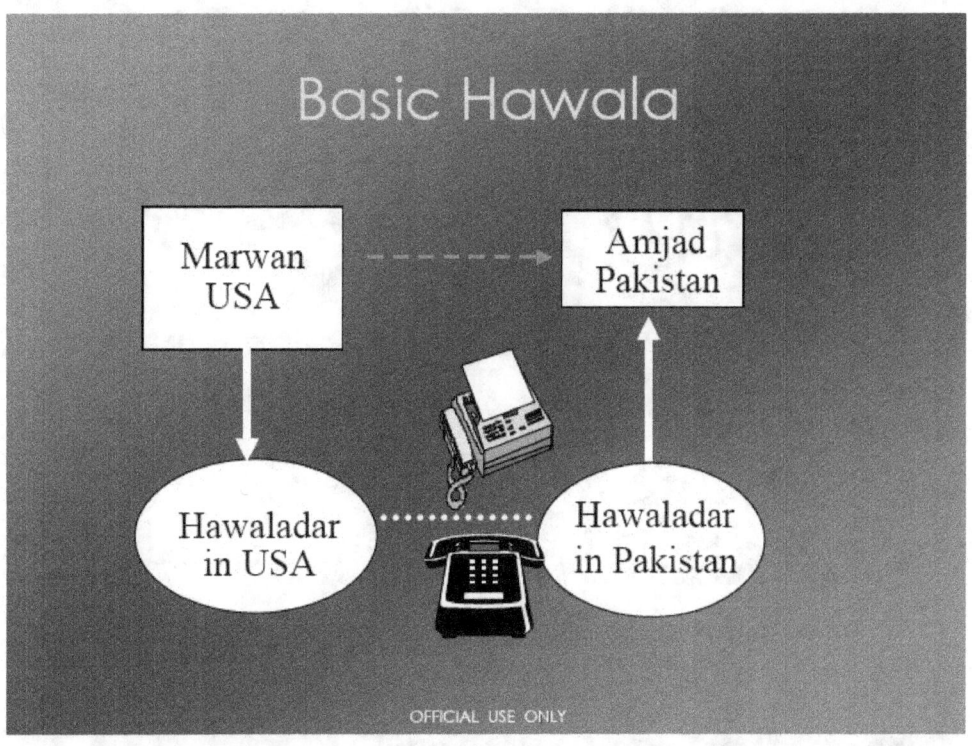

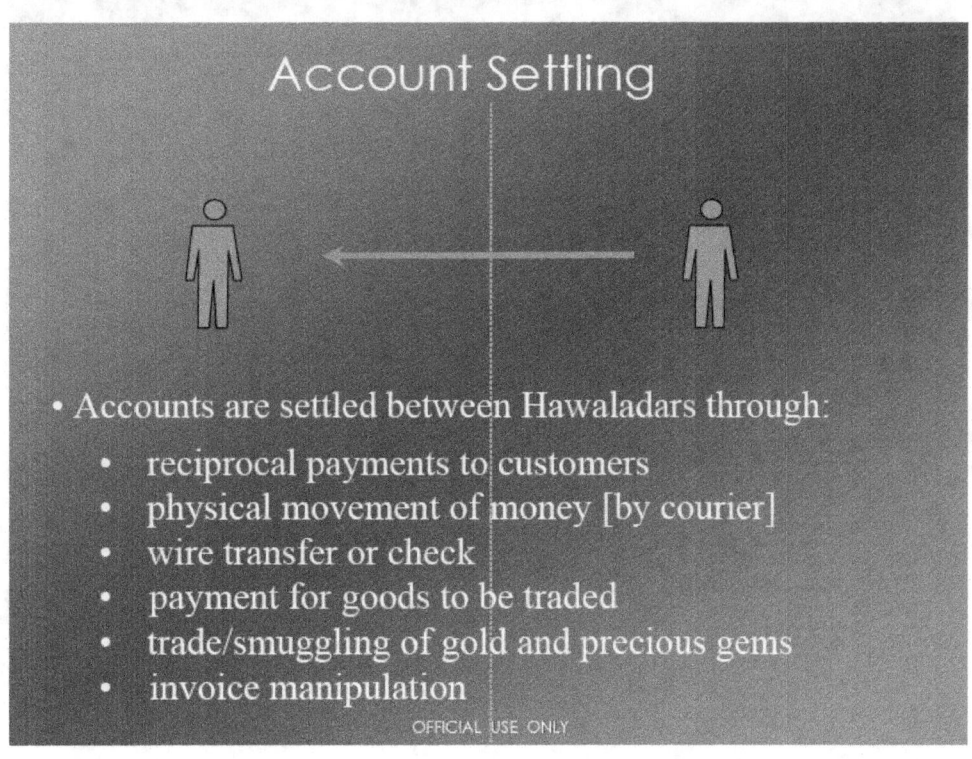

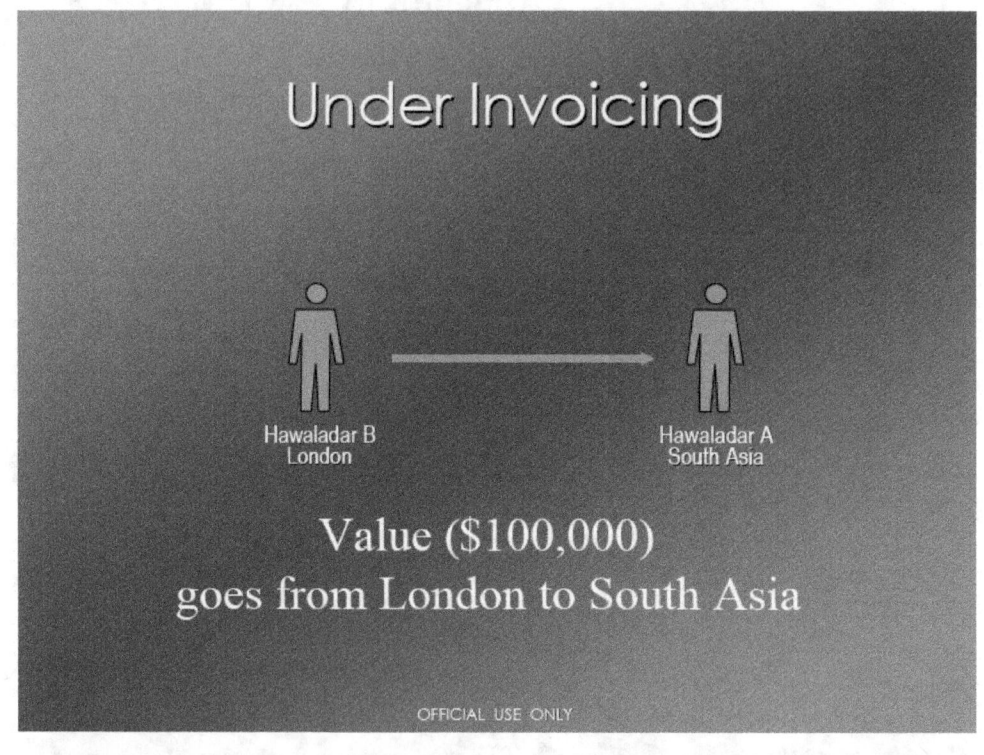

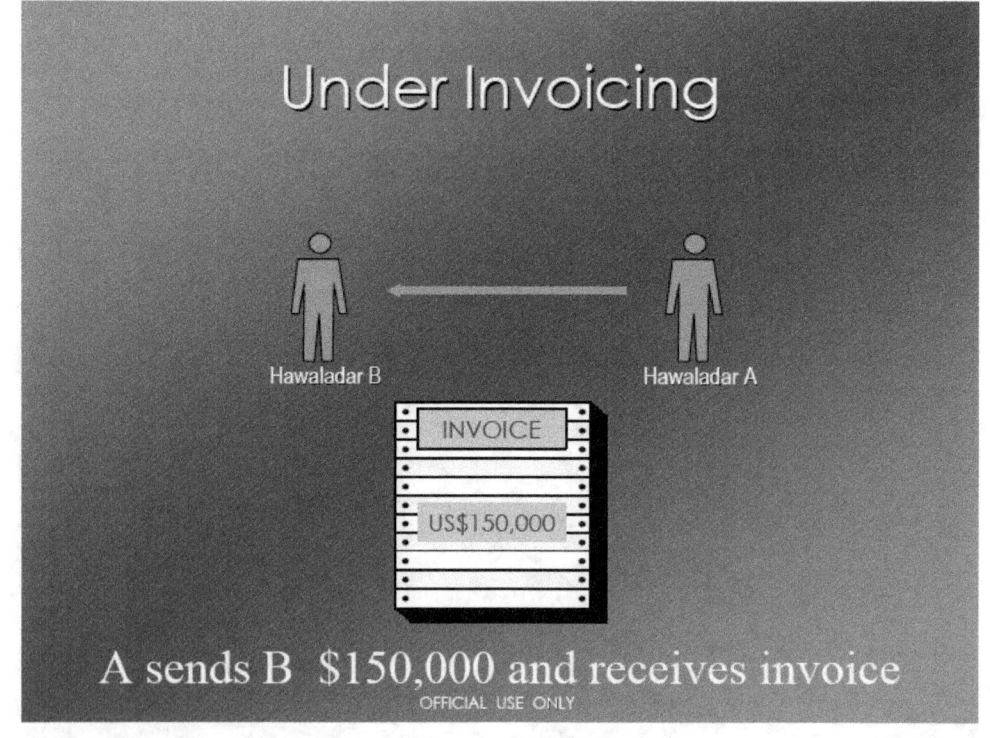

Under Invoicing

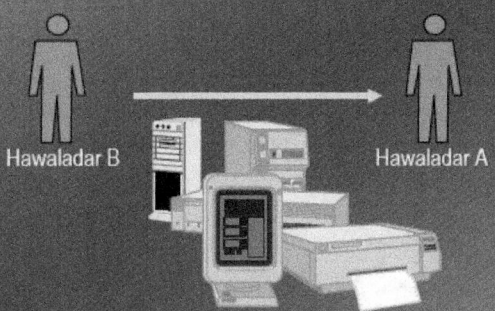

Hawaladar B   Hawaladar A

for $250,000 worth of computer hardware, which balances B's $100,000 debt to A

OFFICIAL USE ONLY

Appendix C

Developing Case Patterns

Examples of IVTS Cases in the United States

During its research on IVTS in the United States, FinCEN met with federal, state, and local law enforcement officials throughout the country to discuss cases being investigated or prosecuted that involve IVTS.[24] Field agents and prosecutors provided FinCEN with extensive cooperation and assistance. Most of the cases highlighted in this report are based on observations of these law enforcement officials. Although many of these investigations are in their preliminary stages, additional criminal activities may become apparent over time.

The IVTS investigations involve a variety of illegal activity, including:

- ❑ use of IVTS providers (unlicensed/unregistered money transmitters) to remit funds to or from abroad (including in several instances an OFAC-blocked country;[25] several illegal hawaladars also connected to drug trafficking);

- ❑ exploitation of cash intensive businesses (e.g., grocery stores; travel agencies; delicatessens; kiosks;[26] convenience stores; phone card businesses; and money exchange businesses) often located in close-knit ethnic communities to launder illicit proceeds derived, for example, from cocaine, heroin, methamphetamine trafficking, alien smuggling, food stamp fraud, and transfer of funds or value to problematic countries (**see graphic below**);

---

[24] Interviews were primarily conducted with representatives of High-Risk Money Laundering and Related Financial Crime Areas (HIFCAs) in Chicago, Los Angeles, San Francisco, New York, and San Juan. Extensive outreach was also conducted with additional contacts beyond the HIFCAs in particular cities where additional leads were discovered (e.g., Washington, D.C. headquarters offices; Atlanta, Georgia; San Diego, California; Charlotte, North Carolina; and Austin, Texas). Also, see Appendix H for a list of all organizations consulted in our study.

[25] The Department of the Treasury's Office of Foreign Assets Control (OFAC) administers and enforces economic and trade sanctions based on United States foreign policy and national security goals against targeted foreign countries, terrorists, international narcotics traffickers, and those engaged in activities related to the proliferation of weapons of mass destruction.

[26] One law enforcement investigation, for example, identified the use of kiosks located in shopping malls and other businesses such as convenience stores to place and layer criminally-derived proceeds. The kiosks were also used by criminal elements as money exchanges. Investigators are focusing on alien smuggling as the underlying unlawful activity.

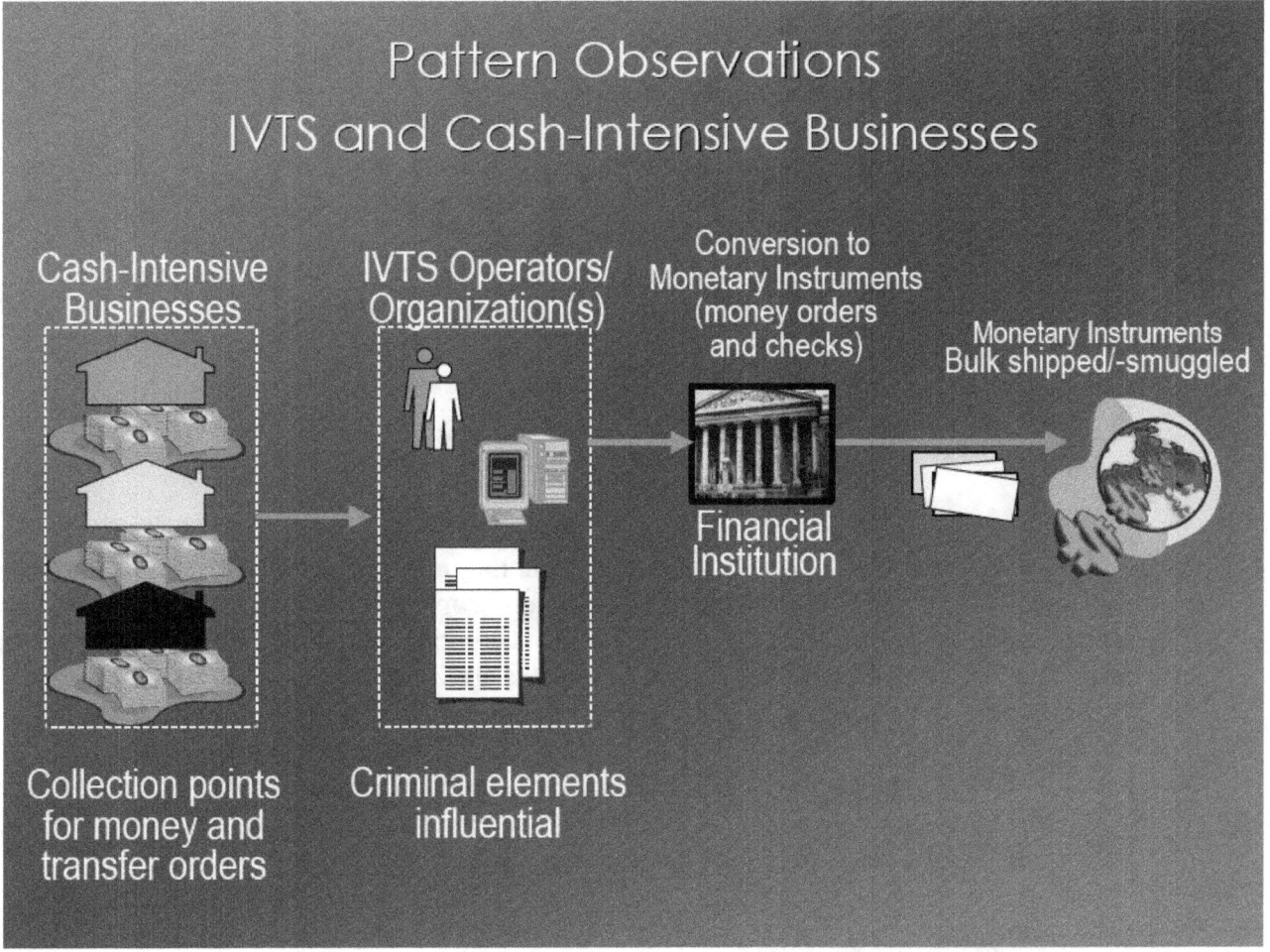

Pattern Observations
IVTS and Cash-Intensive Businesses

Cash-Intensive Businesses — Collection points for money and transfer orders

IVTS Operators/ Organization(s) — Criminal elements influential

Conversion to Monetary Instruments (money orders and checks) — Financial Institution

Monetary Instruments Bulk shipped/-smuggled

- conversion (placement) of bulk cash to money orders and other types of monetary instruments to circumvent federal reporting and recording requirements;

- use of commercial mail carriers to send monetary instruments out of the U.S. to circumvent Currency and Monetary Instrument Report (CMIR) filing requirements;[27]

- use of couriers to smuggle bulk monetary instruments across international borders;

- use of stored value (pre-paid telephone cards) to both transfer value and circumvent reporting requirements;

- exploitation of non-government organizations (NGOs) and charities to move funds potentially linked with terrorist activity;

---

[27] A CMIR is required when a person physically transports currency or other monetary instruments in an aggregate exceeding $10,000 at one time, into or out of the United States. See 31 CFR 103.23(a) and 31 U.S.C. 5316(a) and 5317.

- smuggling of cigarettes; and

- use of Black Market Peso Exchange-type schemes.[28]

In many of the cases, the underlying activity was frequently described as hawala, but FinCEN only has been able to characterize one case as "basic" hawala (i.e., transactions in which a broker or intermediary accepts cash on behalf of a sender in one location, and arranges for disbursement of the cash, minus a small fee, from another broker or intermediary at another location without the actual movement of any funds through any formal financial institution). In most cases, IVTS providers had bank accounts or accounts at other financial institutions, which they used in the settlement of the transactions. This is based on what law enforcement has shared with FinCEN. There may be other "basic" hawalas in the United States that law enforcement has not disclosed or not discovered.

The reality of the IVTS situation in the United States appears to be that many of the investigative cases, along with anecdotal information provided by law enforcement about suspected IVTS involvement in illegal activity (and some information provided by IVTS service providers themselves) indicate a prevalence in the United States of the "mixed" category of IVTS in which illegal money transfer activity is conducted in conjunction with legal business enterprises, such as money transmitters, check cashers, travel agencies, jewelry businesses, grocery stores, and others, and in which settlement is accomplished using the formal financial system. The illegal money transfer activity may encompass both BSA violations and other illegal activities (e.g., narcotics trafficking, alien smuggling fees, and suspected terrorist funding).

Detailed case-related synopses and accompanying graphics of the types of IVTS activity and common patterns observed in the United States are provided below. These cases were reported to FinCEN during consultations with federal and state law enforcement officials. FinCEN will continue to consult with these law enforcement officials to learn additional information and report upon possible subsequent phases and developments. Because most of these cases are still under investigation or raise other sensitive disclosure issues, they have been described generically.

Cases like this require a regulatory and law enforcement infrastructure that will assist law enforcement in identifying the illegal transactions so that a successful prosecution will occur. The challenge for law enforcement is to determine how to target the illegal transactions without affecting the numerous legal transactions by individuals sending money home to their families and without unduly disrupting trade, government, or NGO activities that help those legitimately in need.

---

[28] The Black Market Peso Exchange (BMPE) is a large-scale money laundering system used to launder proceeds of narcotics sales in the United States by Latin American drug cartels by facilitating swaps of dollars in the U.S. for pesos in Colombia through the sale of dollars to Latin American businessmen seeking to buy U.S. goods to export.

Case 1
Suspected Basic IVTS Operation

- ❑ A recent law enforcement investigation identified a non-licensed/registered IVTS operator who provided transfer services to countries in Europe and abroad.
- ❑ The U.S. IVTS operator is a suspected narcotic trafficker.
- ❑ The operator also provided transfer services for customers wishing to send money from an OFAC blocked country located in the Arabian Gulf.
- ❑ The IVTS operator provided his services from his residence.
- ❑ In order to execute payments the operator utilized other IVTS operators in countries abroad in which instructions were provided via fax and phone.
- ❑ Payments were made using a basic hawala system.[29]
- ❑ The operator maintained over $1,000,000 of cash at his residence (believed to be maintained for cash pay-outs).
- ❑ IVTS balances were reconciled through the U.S. IVTS operator meeting with other IVTS operators in Europe.

X.

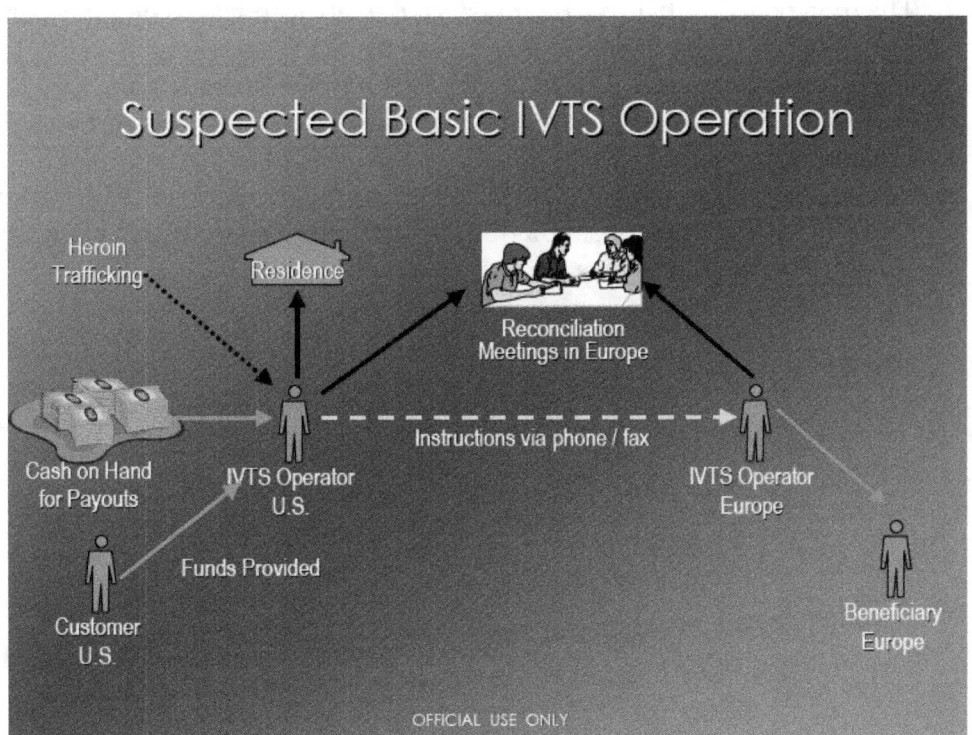

---

[29] Information is subject to change as the case fully develops.

Case 2
Use of Commodities to Reconcile Transfer Payments Between IVTS Operators

- Law enforcement has identified an IVTS operator who provided remittance services to nationals of an East African nation residing in the U.S.
- People wishing to send money would contact the U.S. IVTS operator and arrange to send money to the operator through one of two methods: 1) the person wishing to send money physically provides the funds to the IVTS operator; or 2) the customer deposits the funds to be transferred directly into the operator's account.
- The sender provides the name and phone number of the beneficiary to the operator. The sender also faxes a copy of the deposit receipt to the operator indicating a deposit was made into the operator's account (if that method was used).
- The operator then faxes the payment instructions to his counterpart (family member) located in the East African country. The beneficiary picks up the money from the sender at an exchange business operated by the East African IVTS operator. Funds (proceeds of commodity sales) paid to beneficiaries are withdrawn from a reserve account maintained by the exchange.
- Funds collected by the U.S. IVTS operator were not automatically sent out of the U.S. Usually the U.S. operator would allow the balance of his operating account to accumulate to $10,000.00 before making a wire transfer.
- The money is eventually wire transferred to an account located in a European country that is controlled by the East African IVTS operator.
- The European account is used by the East African operator to purchase goods in bulk that are imported back to the East African national, and further sold at the same location as the exchange.
- Proceeds from the sale of those products are maintained in a reserve account that functions as the primary source for paying money out to beneficiaries from the company's IVTS activities.

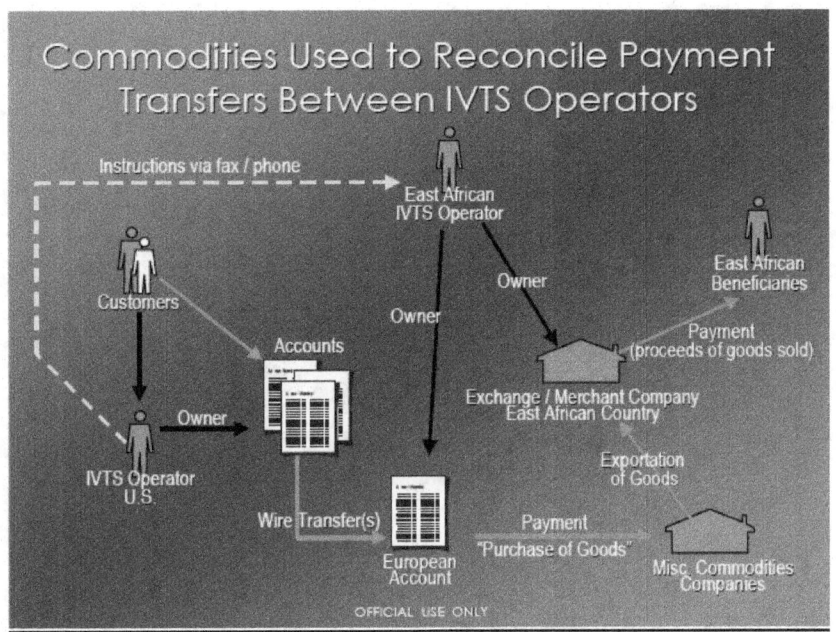

OFFICIAL USE ONLY

XI.

Case 3
Use of Cash Intensive Businesses In Ethnic Communities to Facilitate IVTS Activities, Case A

- Law enforcement efforts identified a case in which an organization provided unlicensed remittance services for nationals of an Arabian Peninsula country residing in the U.S. Numerous businesses within the ethnic community collected money from individuals wishing to send funds back home. A small fee was charged for the transfer services. The funds were then converted to monetary instruments to be smuggled out of the country.
- An agent of the organization would then collect the funds from area delis, travel agencies, and other miscellaneous stores that served as the primary points of contact for people wishing to remit funds.
- The U.S. IVTS operator would then phone and fax all of the transaction orders to another IVTS operator located in the Arabian Peninsula. The beneficiaries would be paid prior to the actual transfer of funds.
- Once cash was collected from the collecting agent of the U.S. organization, several individuals were then enlisted to convert bulk cash to money orders and other types of negotiable instruments. Cash was also structured into nominee bank accounts maintained by area banks. Numerous financial institutions captured some of the structuring activity and subsequently filed SARs.
- Once the cash was converted or deposited into accounts, checks and money orders from the conversion of the funds were provided to couriers who physically smuggled the instruments to the Arabian Peninsula nation.
- Once the Arabian Peninsula IVTS operator received the instruments, he negotiated them through a local bank's correspondent accounted maintained by a U.S. bank.

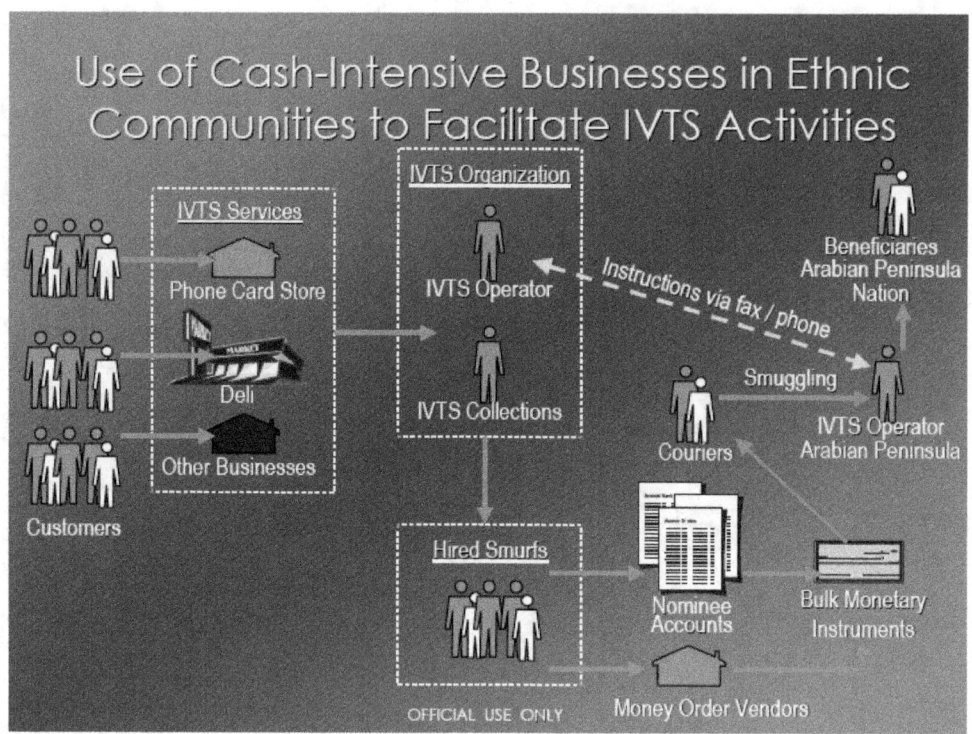

Case 4
Use of Cash Intensive Businesses In Ethnic Communities to Facilitate IVTS Activities, Case B

❏ Law enforcement investigations identified an organization involved in a multitude of criminal activity to include ephedrine trafficking; cocaine, heroin, methamphetamine trafficking; food stamp fraud; resale of stolen property; etc. The organization utilizes numerous businesses and individuals within the ethnic community to facilitate its illegal activities.[30]

❏ The organization also runs a money remitter business that caters to nationals of an Arabian Peninsula country residing in the U.S. The business is unlicensed in the state where it is located and not registered with the federal government.

❏ People wishing to send money through the business contact an agent of the company in which the customer pays the remitter for the service in addition to providing beneficiary information. The U.S. IVTS operator coordinates the payment with his counterpart located in the Arabian Peninsula nation via phone and fax.

---

[30] Based in part on cultural and socio-economic grounds, members of certain ethnic groups mutually support one another in numerous aspects to include financial support in the establishment of businesses. Criminal elements within these ethnic groups also play an active role in supporting the establishment of new businesses through financial support. Thus, the business that is opened with the assistance of funds from criminal organizations becomes vulnerable to facilitating future criminal activity. This can take place as people trusting each other will not always ask about the origin or destination of funds. A blind eye or genuine ignorance can effectively provide cover for activities such as the reselling of stolen goods or the active participation in other illegal activities such as food stamp fraud, coupon fraud, and money laundering.

- Beneficiaries pick up money from the broker located in the Arabian Peninsula nation.
- The actual movement of funds is conducted later when bulk cash is deposited by agents of the organization into personal and business accounts. SARs filed by financial institutions indicate many of those transactions were structured. Money orders and third party checks[31] are also used to deposit funds into accounts or to purchase cashiers checks from financial institutions.
- Funds deposited into accounts owned by the criminal organization in the U.S. were reconciled with the Arabian Peninsula IVTS operator through the use of checks.[32]
- Checks were mailed (via commercial mail) to the IVTS operator located in the Arabian Peninsula nation where they were negotiated through local financial institutions that had correspondent bank accounts with U.S. financial institutions.

---

[31] Law enforcement agents have determined the organization often uses third party checks drawn on other business accounts. The technique includes the purchase of the third party checks by the criminal organization, which are used to purchase cashiers checks from area banks. The use of this technique further complicates the audit trail in identifying the original source of the funds.

[32] The use of checks drawn on respective accounts was the most prominent method used to send money to an African Peninsula Country. It is believed wire transfers were also used as an adaptation resulting from check seizures made by law enforcement during the course of the investigation. Cashiers checks were also used as part of the scheme to reconcile accounts between the criminal organization located in the U.S. and the IVTS operator located in the African Peninsula Country.

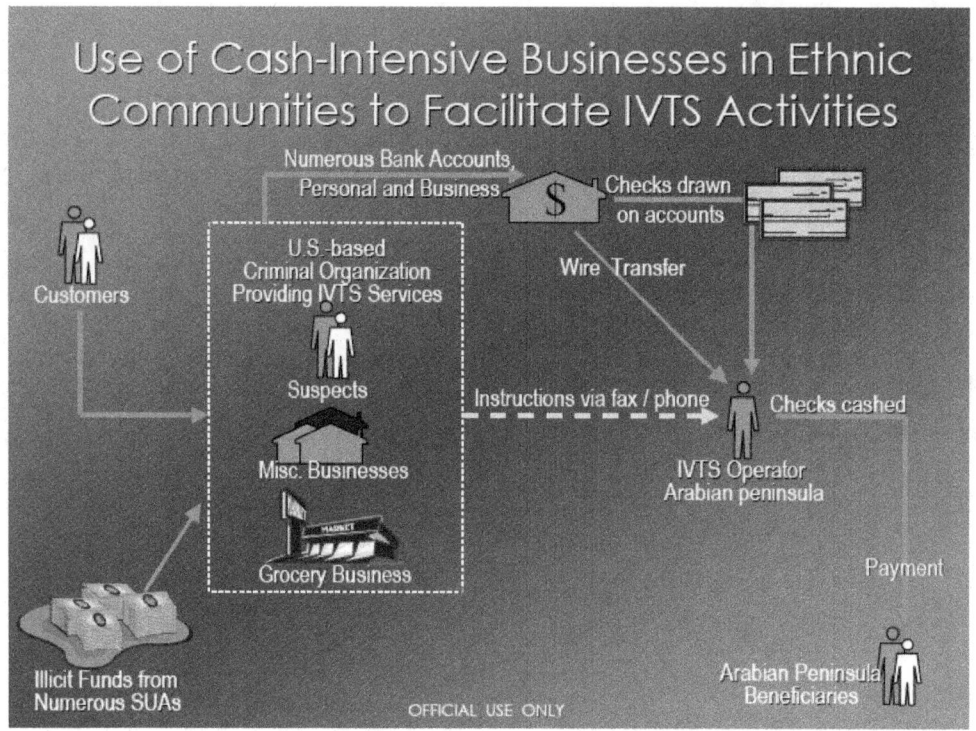

Case 5

Providing Remittance Services to an OFAC Blocked Country

- A U.S. based IVTS organization advertised its services through several different cultural newspapers and the World Wide Web. Those advertisements indicated the company could send money to an OFAC blocked country located in the vicinity of the Arabian Gulf.
- In order to send money through the company the customer would make contact with the IVTS operator and would provide their name and the name and account number of the beneficiary located in the OFAC blocked country.
- There was no commission for the transaction but profit was realized through the exchange rate. The IVTS operator also provided services to known drug traffickers in which a 5% flat fee was charged for moving money derived from criminal activity. The operator was fully aware the money being transferred originated from drug trafficking.
- The operator would then fax instructions to an IVTS operator in the OFAC blocked country in addition to another IVTS operator located in another Arabian Gulf country.
- The IVTS operator located in the OFAC blocked country would provide funds to the beneficiary upon confirmation of the instructions sent by the U.S. IVTS operator.
- Once the U.S. IVTS operator received funds from customers in the U.S. in the form of cash, money orders, and third party checks, the operator would deposit the funds into his account and periodically wire transfer funds to a U.S. based account owned by the IVTS operator operating in the Arabian Gulf country.

34

- The Arabian Gulf IVTS operator would then wire transfer the funds from his U.S. account to another account located in an Arabian Gulf country.
- The money in that account was reconciled with another account located in the OFAC blocked country.
- The U.S. IVTS operator also converted cash into money orders by structuring the purchases of the instruments to circumvent federal identification and recording requirements.
- The U.S. IVTS operator conducted several cash deposits in a manner to possibly circumvent federal recording requirements.[33] The IVTS operator also structured cash to purchase money orders in violation of federal identification and recording requirements.

XII.

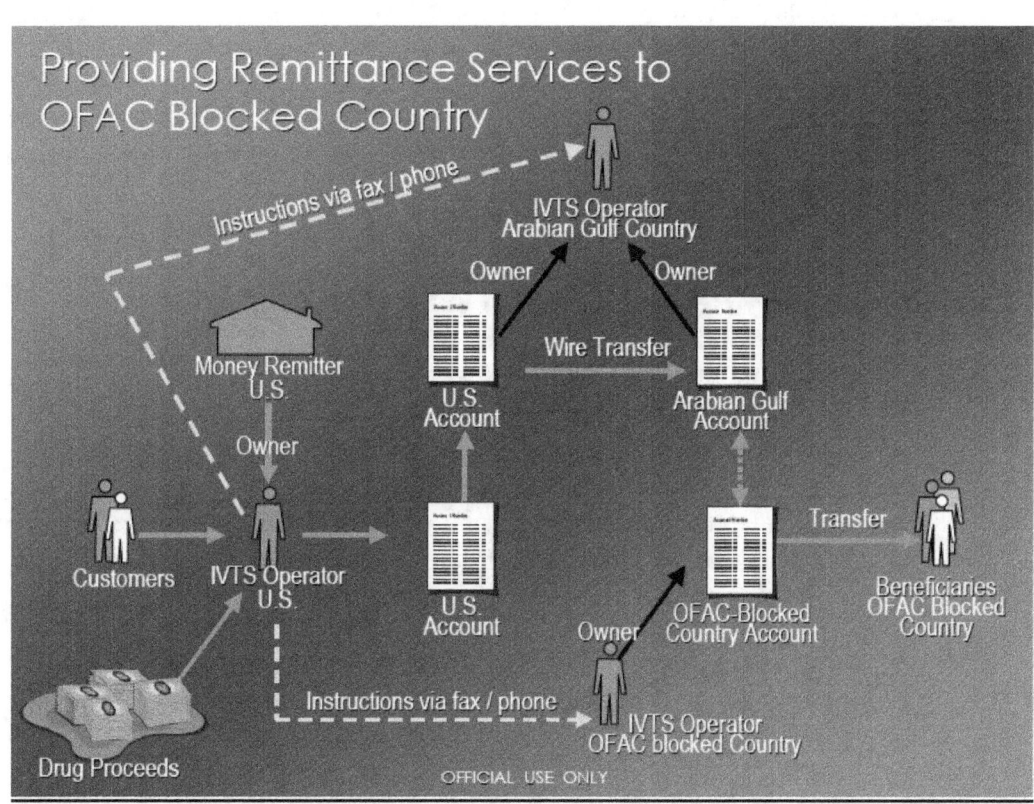

---

[33] Information primarily derived from SAR analysis.

Case 6
Remittance of Bulk Cash Proceeds Derived From Heroin Trafficking

- ❑ Law enforcement agencies of a European country identified a number of storefront companies being used by heroin suspects to launder illicit funds. The storefront companies allegedly provided transfer services to IVTS operators but actually served as placement centers to transfer drug proceeds.
- ❑ The companies used the services of an exchange company located in an Arabian Gulf country as the means to send proceeds from Europe to other criminal elements located in a Southwest Asian country.
- ❑ Bulk cash was collected from drug sales at three storefront operations.
- ❑ Cash was then deposited into business accounts and remitted to the exchange's account maintained by a U.S. owned bank.
- ❑ Funds were then remitted through the exchange to numerous beneficiaries located in other Southwest Asian countries and elsewhere around the world.
- ❑ U.S. financial institutions filed numerous SARs on the exchange company and on subjects and businesses in the U.S. who received or remitted funds from or to the exchange company.[34]

Case 7
East African Money Remitters Located in the United States[35]

- ❑ Law enforcement identified a business located in the U.S. that remits funds on behalf of East African nationals.
- ❑ The business is an unlicensed money transmitter and is not registered with the federal government.
- ❑ SARs indicate continuous structuring of deposits (mostly cash, but sometimes checks and money orders), through the use of multiple individuals into multiple businesses or personal accounts at multiple banks and branches located in multiple states.
- ❑ Suspects made attempts to circumvent CTR requirements.
- ❑ Accounts of suspects with low-income occupations exhibited unusual flows, volumes of funds.
- ❑ Same addresses sometimes being used by multiple suspects.
- ❑ Wire transfers were initiated shortly after deposits were completed funds were then transferred to accounts maintained at banks located in an Arabian Gulf state.
- ❑ Limited knowledge/traceability on the final disbursement of funds once credited to Arabian Gulf banks (black hole syndrome).

---

[34] Several cases have been initiated by U.S. law enforcement on a number of U.S. based subjects believed to have done business with the exchange company.
[35] Information primarily derived from SAR analysis.

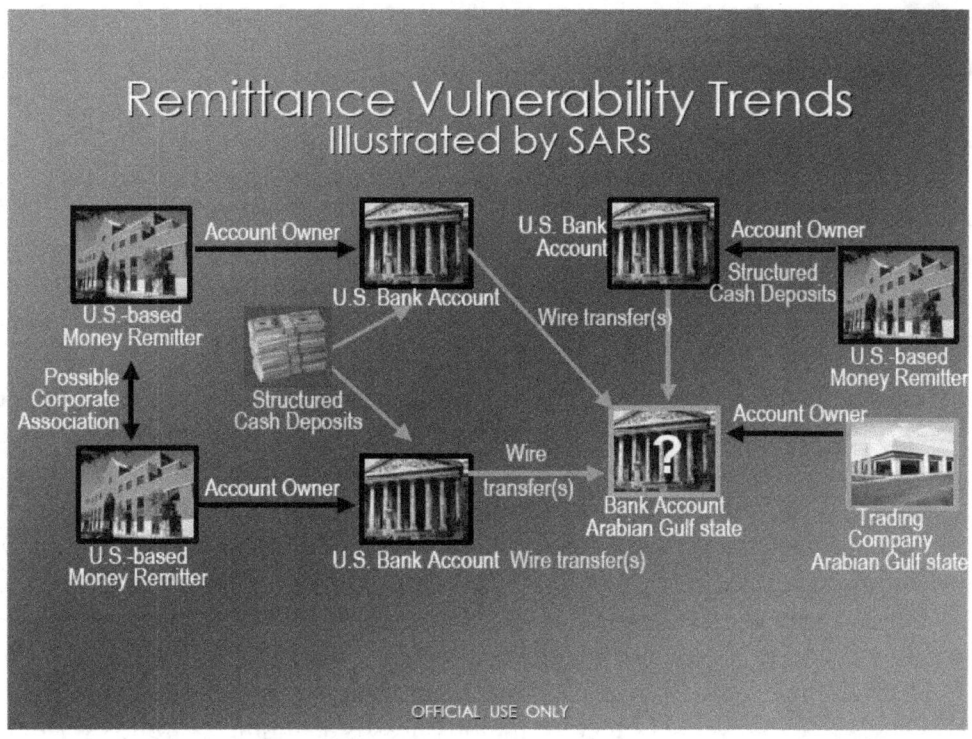

Case 8

Providing Remittance Services to an OFAC Blocked Country

- ❏ A law enforcement investigation identified six unlicensed money remitters.
- ❏ Investigative efforts identified several of the remitters as possibly remitting funds on behalf of known criminal elements.
- ❏ Investigations are pending to determine if any of the companies violated federal law by remitting funds to OFAC blocked countries.[36]
- ❏ Extensive ledgers were maintained by the entities detailing wire transfer activity.
- ❏ The companies guaranteed money transmission to the OFAC blocked country within 1-4 days.
- ❏ The only beneficiary information required to complete a transaction from the companies was the name and bank account number of the recipient oversees. Select businesses also provided hand delivery of funds to beneficiaries for an additional charge.

---

[36] A full financial analysis of the bank records associated with the case is still pending. However, many of the advertisements posted by the suspect companies indicated they provided transfer services from the U.S. to an OFAC blocked country located in the Arabian Gulf.

Case 9
United States v. Mohamed M. Hussein, et al.

- ❑ A law enforcement investigation identified an illegal remitter in Boston, MA, that provided foreign transmittal services. The business operated without a license in violation of MA State law.
- ❑ On August 7, 2000, the president of the company filed an application with the commonwealth of MA, Division of Bank and Loan Agencies, in order to obtain a license to engage in the business of receiving deposits of money for transmission to foreign countries.
- ❑ The application identified another business located in an Arabian Gulf country as an affiliate of the company. The application also included a number of receipts indicating the business had already remitted funds internationally. In response, the Division of Banks sent a letter to the business advising the company of their obligation to obtain a state license, not to continue to engage in illegal wire transmission activities, and the penalties if the activity continued. Two subsequent letters were also sent to agents of the company with little or no response.
- ❑ Agents of the company engaged in the deposit of cash and checks originating from several subjects located in MA and other states.
- ❑ Once deposits were credited to the businesses account, the funds were then wired to an Arabian Gulf country in which the wired funds were made available to the designated recipient.
- ❑ Agents would typically initiate wire transfers telephonically through an automated wire transfer procedure that did not require the agent to speak to a bank employee. Nearly $3,000,000 was wired oversees through the illegal wire transmitter.
- ❑ Checks were also written from the remitter account for recipients receiving money from oversees senders residing in the United States.
- ❑ On July 22, 2002, Mohamed HUSSEIN, an agent of the business, was sentenced to one and half years in prison and two years of supervised release for operating an illegal money transmitting operation without a state license. Another subject, Liban HUSSEIN, president of the company, has also been charged in the case.

Case 10
Charitable Organization With Possible Links to a Designated Terrorist Organization Remitting Funds Abroad[37]

- ❑ Law enforcement investigations identified possible links between the owners of a U.S. based charitable foundation and a designated terrorist organization.
- ❑ A central account was used by agents of the company to deposit cash. Several SARs were filed by financial institutions on the suspect nature of the transactions.
- ❑ International wire transactions were then initiated from the account in which funds were sent to Russia and two former Soviet Republic States.
- ❑ Wire transfers were also credited to the U.S. company account from unknown transactors through a European Bank.

---

[37] Information primarily derived from SAR analysis.

- The U.S. company also wire-transferred funds to another U.S. based business engaged in similar business activities (charity). All of these transactions are suspect based on the volume and patterns of activity affecting the company's account vis-a-vis the types of services the company was providing.
- Wire transfers from the company were credited to a similar type of U.S. based company. That company also is suspected of having an association with a designated terrorist organization.

Case 11
IVTS Activities Conducted on Behalf of Known Criminal Elements

- Law enforcement identified an extensive IVTS network that provided remittance services and laundered drug proceeds on behalf of a Middle Eastern drug trafficking organization.
- U.S. financial institutions identified both deposit and transfer activity conducted by agents of the IVTS organization and subsequently filed SARs on the large cash deposits conducted by numerous transactors.
- The network sent money throughout the world through the use of wire transfer payments.

Case 12
Use of Money Orders to Facilitate IVTS Activities[38]

- Law enforcement officials initiated an investigation based on SAR referrals that identified the negotiation of bulk money orders through a bank located in a Middle Eastern country.
- The money orders appeared to have been purchased at various money order vendors located in the U.S.
- Money orders were then negotiated through a bank located in a Middle Eastern country and ultimately cleared through a U.S. correspondent account.
- It is unknown how the money orders were transported to the Middle East but it is assumed that they were smuggled based on the large volume negotiated.
- There are indications of ethnic crossovers in facilitating money transfers.

Case 13
Use of Money Orders to Facilitate Black Market Peso Exchange (BMPE)

- Law enforcement identified a BMPE case in which money orders were heavily used to convert drug proceeds to negotiable instruments.
- The organization in the U.S. worked under the direction of a money broker located in a Central American country. It is believed the money broker would provide instructions to his agents in the U.S. regarding the pick-up of bulk cash derived from narcotics trafficking.

---

[38] Information primarily derived from SAR analysis.

- Once the cash was picked up, subjects within the organization would immediately convert the cash to money orders. The money orders were purchased from area vendors in a manner to circumvent federal reporting and recording requirements.
- Agents of the company also structured cash into bank accounts.
- Once drug proceeds were converted, the Central American broker provided his U.S. agents with coded instructions on the distribution of the funds. Much of the funds were distributed via commercial mail carriers to various U.S. companies on behalf of customers doing business with the Central American broker.[39]
- Some of the funds were also mailed via commercial carrier or smuggled via courier to the Central American broker where they were further negotiated by third parties.

Case 14
Use of Black Market Brokers, Bank Accounts, and Shell Companies
United States of America v. Maria Carolina NOLASCO, et al.

- A recent law enforcement investigation identified a bank official working in the private banking department of an institution in the Northeast U.S. facilitated the transfer of hundreds of millions of dollars in less than a year by using the facilities of the U.S. bank. The money transfer operations required a license under State law and federal registration, neither of which had taken place. The transfers were between the U.S. and a South American country.
- Money brokers sent the bank official instructions by fax for transfers to be conducted through dozens of accounts [the official controlled more than 250 accounts].
- The bank official also controlled accounts of more than 40 shell companies.
- Wire transfers out of these accounts were payments for goods bought by other companies, which had purchased the dollars through the black market.
- The bank official used the bank's wire facilities to make the transfers [instructions given to the wire facility also by fax from the bank employee].
- The money transferred appears to be the proceeds of illegal drug trafficking.

Case 15
Cigarette Smuggling in Support of Terrorist Organizations
United States of America v. Mohamad Youssef Hammoud, et al.

- Law enforcement efforts identified a U.S. cell of a known Middle Eastern terrorist group that engaged in cigarette smuggling.
- Subjects from the U.S. based cell acquired numerous credit cards to purchase cigarettes in bulk from various cigarette wholesalers.
- Once purchased the cigarettes were transported to another state within the U.S. with a significantly higher excise tax than the state where the cigarettes were purchased.
- The cigarettes were sold for profit to a central contact.
- A senior member of the U.S. based cell often communicated with members of a similar cell operating in another North American country. That cell was identified

---

[39] The purchase of U.S. dollars by Central American businessmen who wished to get a better exchange rate of pesos to dollars.

by law enforcement as acquiring equipment (with possible military applications) on behalf of a known Middle Eastern terrorist organization.

❑ A senior member of the U.S. based cell at least on one occasion transferred funds to a member of the other terrorist cell located in another North American country.

Case 16
Use of Phone Cards to Transfer Value

❑ Law enforcement efforts identified a criminal organization that used pre-paid phone cards to front money for a drug transaction.[40] The phone cards were also used to circumvent CMIR requirements.[41]

---

[40] The purpose of the initial drug transaction was to prove to drug traffickers the criminal organization had the funds (value of the phone cards) to purchase drugs from the drug trafficking organization.
[41] As per current federal law, phone cards are not required to be reported on CMIRs despite having a total value in excess of $10,000.00.

Appendix D

International Oversight Practices

International Oversight Practices Relating to Hawala

Oversight of hawala operations vary from country to country, ranging from prohibition, to various degrees of regulation, to doing nothing. Many countries in which immigrant communities remit money to their homelands generally treat hawala as a matter of regulation and scrutiny, even more so after the attacks of September 11, 2001. In the past, hawala was regarded as a means of transferring money that caused concern only when it facilitated the commission of a crime. The United States, Canada, the United Kingdom, and other European countries fall into this category. Recently, many jurisdictions have introduced regulations requiring the registration and/or licensing of all money transfer businesses that include hawala and other IVTS.

It is essential to note that, because the term hawala means 'transfer,' it is used in some Middle Eastern countries as synonymous to formal money transfers through banks or wire transfers. For example, in Saudi Arabia, where there is formal hawala, people mostly use the term 'hundi' to denote informal money transfers. Because of the strict enforcement of Saudi laws prohibiting hundi practices, most expatriates there apparently send remittances through bank channels, the services of which have improved substantially in recent times.

Similarly, Japan authorizes only banks to engage in funds transfers and criminalizes other methods. Because illicit transfers there often take place through banks, Japanese authorities have provided guidelines to financial institutions for better reporting of suspicious activities to the Financial Intelligence Office.

Australia, Germany, and Hong Kong stand out as jurisdictions with large immigrant populations that have long-standing regulations that apply to hawala and other money transfer businesses. They each require the licensing of businesses that remit money. Australia's Financial Transaction Reports Act of 1988 also requires that remittance agents report suspicious transactions and cash transactions over A$10,000 to the authorities. AUSTRAC, the Australian equivalent of FinCEN, has also engaged in an outreach program to inform remittance agents of the rules and their obligations.

Hong Kong enacted legislation in June 2000 requiring money transfer agents to register with the authorities, establish the identity of their customers, keep the records of transactions over HK$20,000, keep those records for six years, and report suspicious transactions. An outreach program was also part of the strategy, including the publication and distribution of guidelines and notifications to those concerned (including travelers who might act as money couriers).

In Germany, under legislation enacted in 2000, providers of financial services "commercially or on a scale which requires a commercially organized business undertaking," must obtain a license from the Federal Banking Supervisory Office. Both money transfer businesses (including "non-account related" money transfers) and foreign exchange bureaus are considered as financial services requiring a license.

In the United Kingdom, during November 2001, anti-money laundering regulations came into effect, which require money services businesses, such as bureaux de change and money remitters, to register with HM Customs and Excise. In addition, HM Customs was given new powers to enter and inspect such businesses, including hawala and other IVTS, to ensure compliance with the rules. Before this legislation, the main legal instrument regulating money transfer businesses was the 1993 Money Laundering Regulations. Theoretically, unregistered IVTS were subject to the 1993 regime. However, in practice no enforcement action would have been taken without another substantive offense, such as drug money laundering. This practice continues to be the focus of law enforcement efforts in the UK to date.

Countries on the receiving end of workers' remittances are sometimes jurisdictions with controls on capital flows and currency exchange rates. These include Pakistan, India, Sri Lanka, and others. While hawala enables expatriates to help their families in their homeland, it also facilitates tax evasion, evasion of exchange controls, capital flight, and corruption. Combined with false invoicing, gold, or precious stones smuggling, the capital flow can actually be negative for such regions. As hawaladars allow for the draining of financial resources and deprivation of highly valued foreign currency in those countries, hawala has been outlawed for some time both in India and Pakistan. In spite of these legal restrictions, the hawala business thrives in both nations.

In India, the Foreign Exchange Management Act (FEMA) of May 2000 has replaced the Foreign Exchange Regulation Act of 1973 (FERA). The old law had criminalized the practice of hawala, and carried penalties of up to three years in prison for amounts less than 100,000 Indian rupees, seven years in prison for higher amounts, and fines up to five times the amount involved. Under the new law, hawala is a civil offense carrying a penalty of up to three times the amount involved. However, legal action is often difficult to pursue due to the general lack of evidence. The money seized may be confiscated under both Acts.

In Pakistan, only banks can conduct money transfers, although the State Bank announced in the summer of 2002 that it intended to authorize money changers also to engage in fund transfers. Under the proposed plan, some money changers may be issued Exchange Company Licenses. Details of how these would be regulated are not yet available.

Following the Abu Dhabi conference in May 2002 on hawala, sponsored by the United Arab Emirates (UAE) Central Bank, the UAE seemed ready to provide the lead in

introducing a regulatory regime that would take into consideration the views and interests of hawaladars, their competitors, and the clients of hawala in the Gulf region. As of November 4, 2002, the central bank of the UAE began registering brokers of informal overseas money transfers known as hawala in a bid to curb money laundering.

Appendix E

Acknowledgments

1. California Department of Financial Institutions
2. California Department of Justice
3. Central Intelligence Agency
4. Coral Gables Florida Police Department
5. Drug Enforcement Administration
6. El Dorado Task Force (New York/New Jersey)
7. Federal Bureau of Investigation
8. Federal Reserve Bank of New York
9. Federal Reserve Board
10. Financial Crimes Enforcement Network
11. Financial Review Group (Federal Bureau of Investigation)
12. Federal Law Enforcement Training Center
13. High Intensity Drug Trafficking Areas (HIDTA)
    a. Atlanta, GA
    b. Chicago, IL
    c. New York/New Jersey
14. High-Risk Money Laundering and Related Financial Crime Areas (HIFCA)
    a. Chicago, IL
    b. Los Angeles, CA
    c. New York/New Jersey
    d. San Francisco, CA
    e. San Juan, PR
15. Immigration & Naturalization Service
16. Internal Revenue Service (Criminal Investigation Division; Compliance Division)
17. International Monetary Fund
18. Los Angeles Police Department
19. Miami-Dade Police Department
20. National Drug Intelligence Center
21. National Security Council
22. New York City Police Department
23. New York County District Attorney's Office
24. Office of Foreign Assets Control
25. Operation Green Quest (United States Customs Service)
26. State of New York Banking Department
27. State of New York Office of Attorney General
28. State of Texas Office of Attorney General
29. United Kingdom
    a. HM Customs & Excise
    b. National Crime Squad
    c. National Criminal Intelligence Service

      d. National Investigation Service
30. United States Attorney's Office
      a. Atlanta, GA
      b. Charlotte, NC
      c. Los Angeles, CA
      d. Newark, NJ
      e. San Diego, CA
      f. Washington, DC
      g. U.S. Virgin Islands
31. United States Customs Service
32. United States Department of Agriculture
33. United States Department of Justice
34. United States Department of Labor
35. United States Department of State
36. United States Department of the Treasury
37. United States Postal Inspection Service
38. United States Secret Service
39. United Nations Monitoring Group
40. World Bank

The research group would like to thank member nation Financial Intelligence Units (FIUs) of the Egmont Group who responded to our IVTS Survey.

We would also like to acknowledge the assistance and expertise provided by Professor Nikos Passas of Temple University. His contributions were invaluable to the research conducted in the study.

Seminars Associated with the IVTS Study

On May 15, 2002, FinCEN assisted in a presentation at the UAE Hawala Seminar held at Abu Dhabi, United Arab Emirates. And on May 25, 2002, FinCEN gave a presentation at the Institute of Banking Studies Money Laundering Seminar held in Kuwait City, Kuwait. Both seminars drew hundreds of attendees from government agencies – both regulatory and law enforcement – and the private sector. Many in attendance were able to share with FinCEN their perspectives and recommendations regarding the challenges posed by IVTS.

FinCEN's Office of Strategic Analysis, Non-Traditional Methodologies Branch, hosted a Hawala Seminar on May 29, 2002. Fifty-five attendees representing seventeen agencies participated in this seminar.

On October 9, 2002, FinCEN hosted an international conference for the Egmont Group Financial Intelligence Units on IVTS and international observations, challenges, and enhanced coordination of counter measures.

www.ingramcontent.com/pod-product-compliance
Lightning Source LLC
Chambersburg PA
CBHW080620290526

45790CB00007B/2861